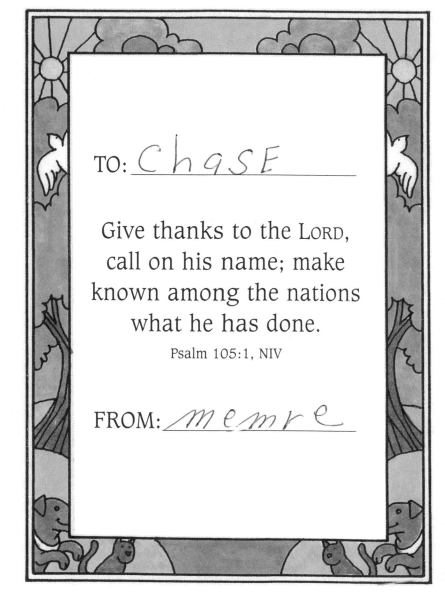

TO: Chase

Give thanks to the LORD,
call on his name; make
known among the nations
what he has done.

Psalm 105:1, NIV

FROM: memre

Little Prayers for Little Ones
Copyright ©1995
by the Zondervan Corporation

ISBN 0-310-97173-X

Project Editor: Jesslyn DeBoer
Design: Anne Huizenga
Illustrations: Comark Group
Layout: Mark Veldheer

Made in United States of America
98 99 00 / Q / 9 8 7 6 5

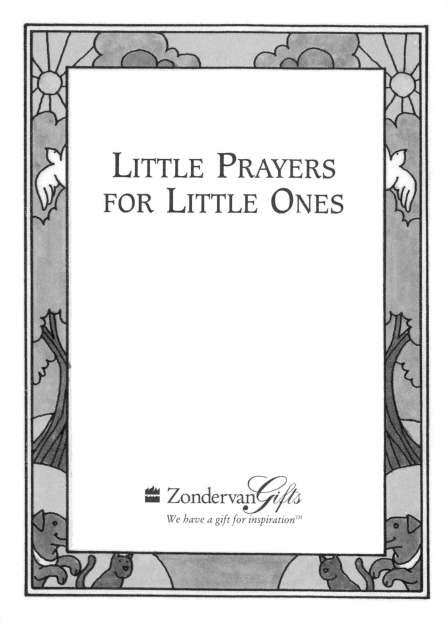

LITTLE PRAYERS
FOR LITTLE ONES

Zondervan*Gifts*

We have a gift for inspiration™

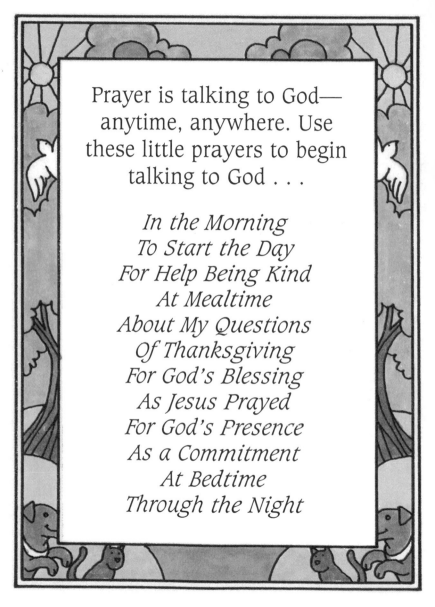

Prayer is talking to God—anytime, anywhere. Use these little prayers to begin talking to God . . .

In the Morning
To Start the Day
For Help Being Kind
At Mealtime
About My Questions
Of Thanksgiving
For God's Blessing
As Jesus Prayed
For God's Presence
As a Commitment
At Bedtime
Through the Night

A Little Prayer
In the Morning

Dear God–
I wake up in the
morning

and outside my
window
I hear and see
squirrels,
birds, and dogs;
cats, cars, and trees.

I remember you
made all these . . .

and that you made
this day for me.

Thank you, God.

Amen.

A Little Prayer
To Start the Day

Lord,
as I go out today

be with me and
bless my play.

Guide the things I do
and say,

And lead me in
your loving way.

Amen.

A LITTLE PRAYER
FOR HELP
BEING KIND

Dear Lord–
Help me be patient,
loving and good.

Help me to be the
friend I should.

Help me learn to
share my toys.

And help me
be kind
to other girls
and boys.

Amen.

A LITTLE PRAYER
AT MEALTIME

To thank the Lord,
I bow my head

and think of apples,
milk, and bread.

I remember
God is good,

And I thank him
for my food.

Amen.

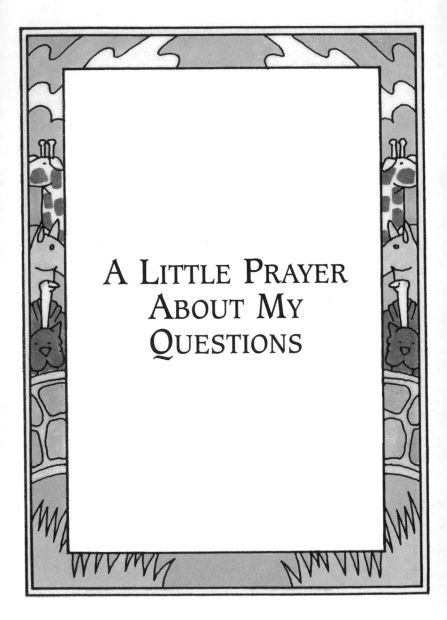

A LITTLE PRAYER
ABOUT MY
QUESTIONS

Lord,
where do the birds
go when they fly?

How do the clouds
stay up in the sky?

How did you think
of red, yellow,
and blue?

. . . and all the
animals in the zoo?

Why do the
mountains stand
so tall?

And how does the
rain know when
to fall?

When will I
grow up? And what
will I be?

Lord, please send
your answers to me.

Amen.

A LITTLE PRAYER
OF THANKSGIVING

Thank you,
God,
for all things
good . . .

for home and
clothes and
tasty food.

Thank you for
my family and
all the love they
show to me.

Thank you for my
friends and toys

and for each day
you fill with joy.

Amen.

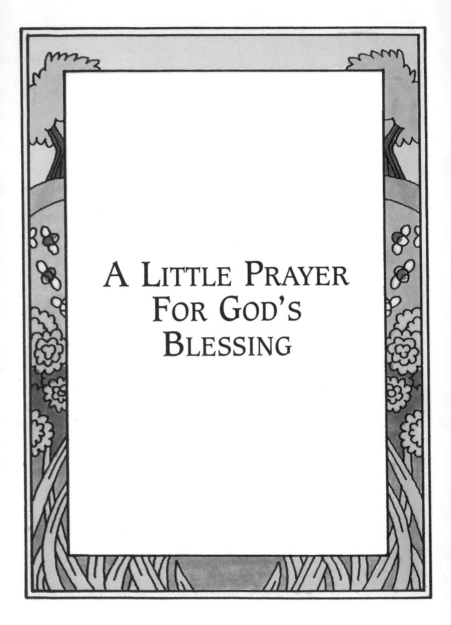

A Little Prayer
For God's
Blessing

God bless the
plants and bless
the trees.

God bless the
birds, kittens, ants,
and bees.

God bless my
friends and family.

And please, dear God, also bless me.

Amen.

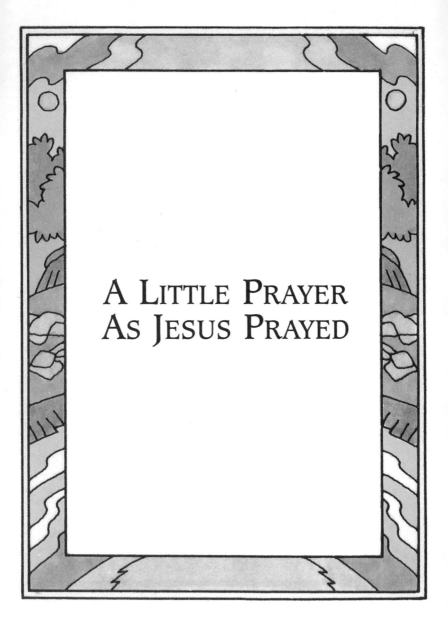

A LITTLE PRAYER
AS JESUS PRAYED

Our Father
in heaven,
hallowed be your
name,
your kingdom come,
your will be done
on earth as it is
in heaven.

Give us today our daily bread. Forgive us our debts, as we also have forgiven our debtors.

And lead us not
into temptation,
but deliver us from
the evil one.

For yours is the
kingdom,
and the power,
and the glory
forever.

Amen.

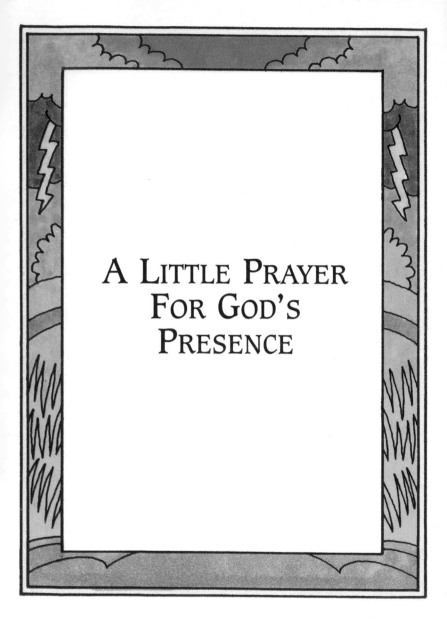

A LITTLE PRAYER
FOR GOD'S
PRESENCE

Dear God,
There are times
I feel sad,
then I know
you are there.
There are times
I'm afraid,
and I know
that you care.

There are times
when I'm happy,
then I know
you are glad.
There are times
when I hurt,
and I know that
you're sad.

So whatever
may happen–
whatever may be,

I'll always
remember that
you love me.

Amen.

A Little Prayer
As a Commitment

Lord,
You want me to
praise you–
I will!

You want me to
read the Bible–
I will!
You want me to
help people–
I will!

You want me to be
your special friend—

I WILL!

Amen.

A Little Prayer
At Bedtime

Dear Jesus,
As I go to bed,
send sweet dreams
to fill my head.

Keep me safe
tonight I pray,
and wake me to a
brand new day.

Amen.

A Little Prayer
Through
the Night

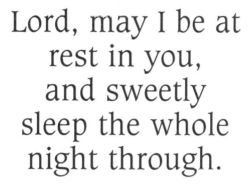

Lord, may I be at
rest in you,
and sweetly
sleep the whole
night through.

Refresh my strength
for your own sake,
so I may serve you
when I wake.

Amen.